BOSTON

GUITAR ANTHOLOGY SERIES

Transcribed by STEVE PEPLIN

Project Manager: COLGAN BRYAN
Project Coordinator: SHERYL ROSE
Book Design: JOSEPH KLUCAR
Art Layout: MICHAEL RAMSAY

Cover Art

BOSTON
© 1976 CBS Inc.

DON'T LOOK BACK
© 1978 CBS Inc.

THIRD STAGE
© 1986 MCA Records, Inc.

Third Stage

MW01198824

CONTENTS

AMANDA

Words and Music by
TOM SCHOLZ

Guitar solo
w/Rhy. Fig. 2 & Fill 1

8

DON'T BE AFRAID

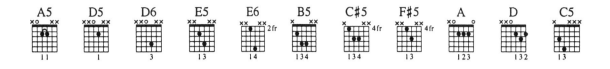

Words and Music by
TOM SCHOLZ

Don't Be Afraid - 6 - 1

Don't Be Afraid - 6 - 6

DON'T LOOK BACK

Words and Music by
TOM SCHOLZ

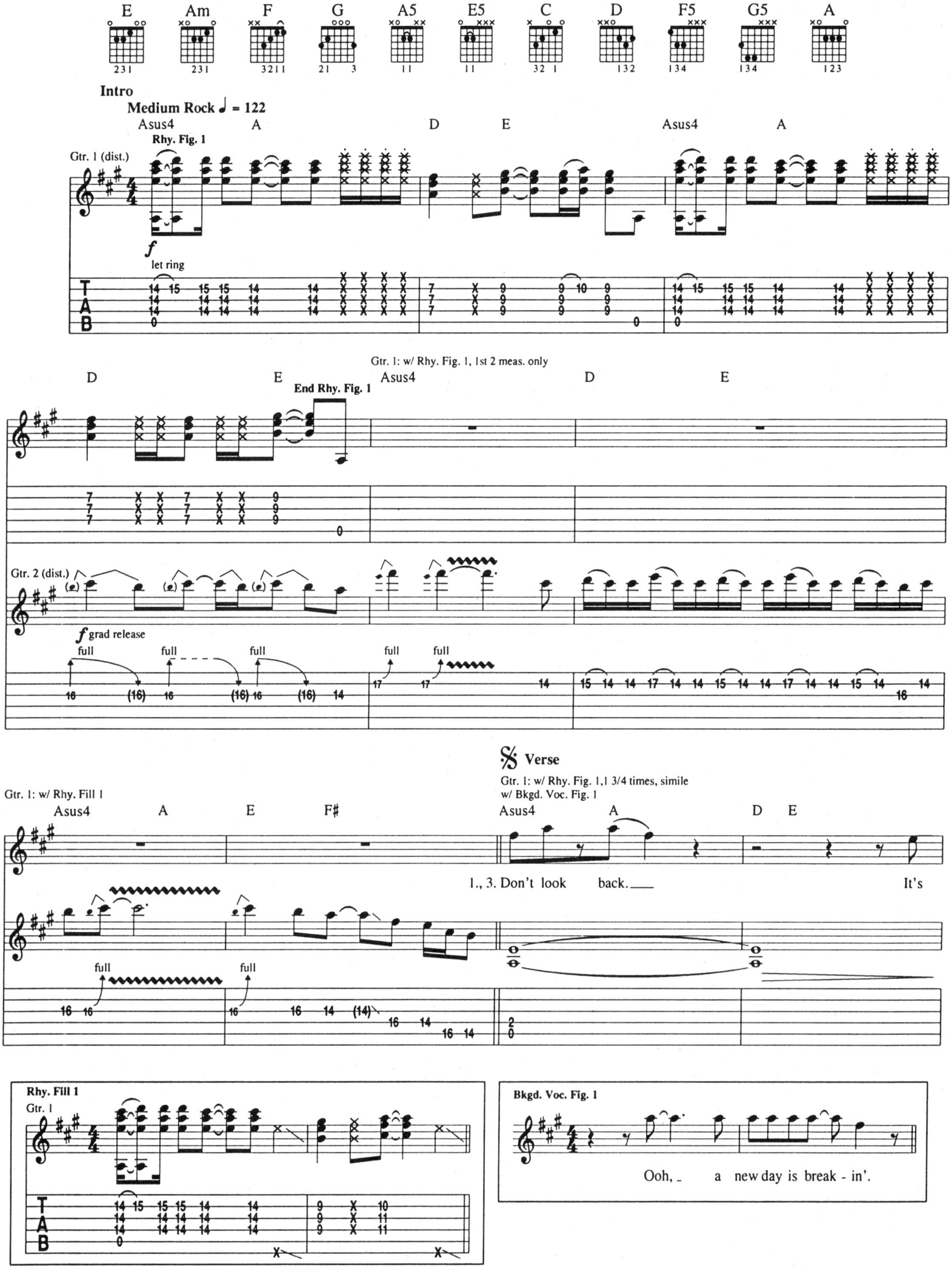

Yes I will! Come on! ___ I fin-

'ly see the dawn ar-riv-in'. I see ___

___ be-yond the road I'm driv-in'.

Breakdown
Gtr. 1: w/ Rhy. Fig. 1
Gtr. 3 tacet

Verse
Gtr. 1: w/ Rhy. Fig. 1, 1 1/2 times
w/ Bkgd. Voc. Fig. 3
Gtr. 2 tacet.

2. It's a bright hor-i-zon. Oh, I
(And I'm a-wake, ___ I ___

pitch: A

Bkgd. Voc. Fig. 3

Ooh. ___

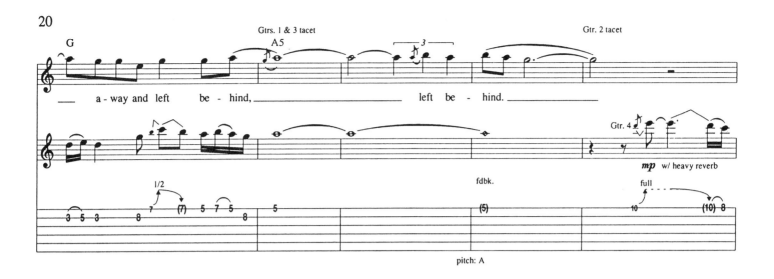

a - way and left be - hind, _____ left be - hind. _____

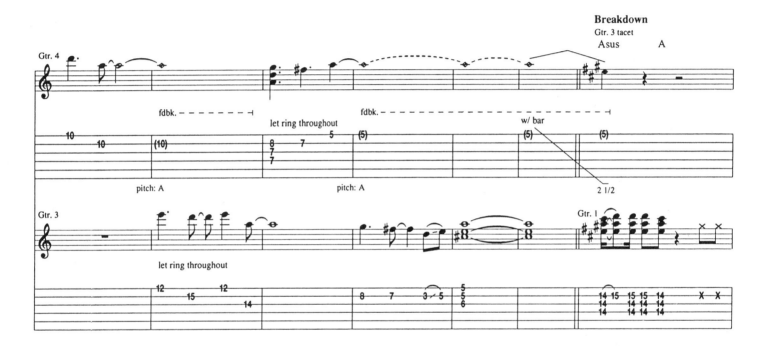

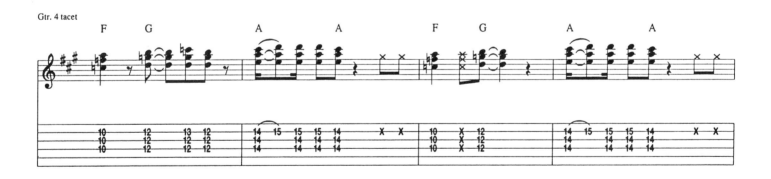

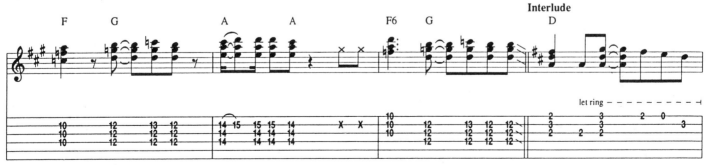

*Doubled w/ 12 str. acous.

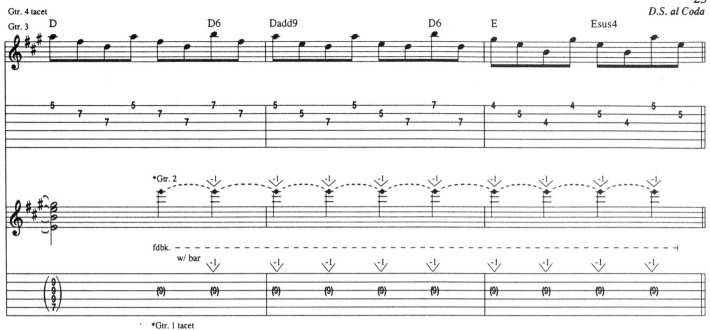

⊕ *Coda*

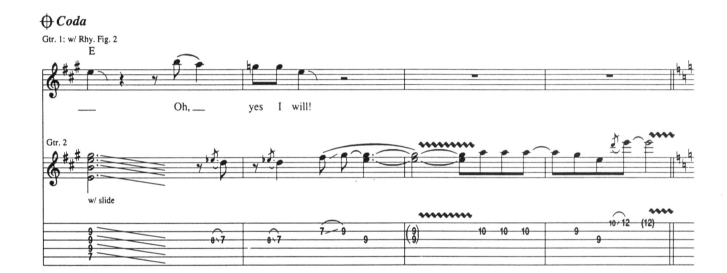

Oh, — yes I will!

Chorus

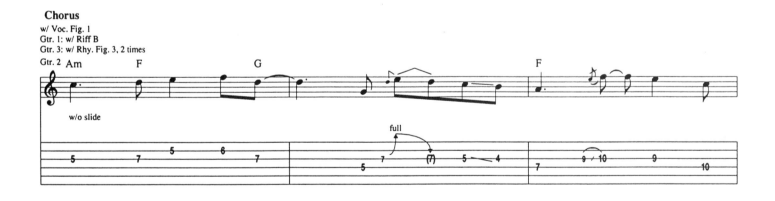

Don't Look Back - 10 - 10

FEELIN' SATISFIED

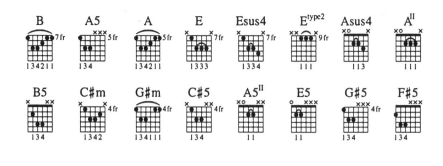

Words and Music by
TOM SCHOLZ

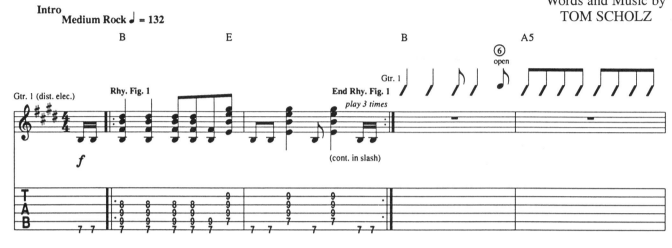

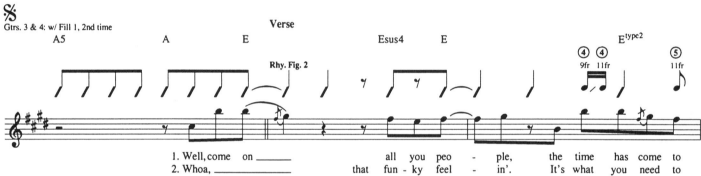

1. Well, come on _____ all you peo - ple, the time has come to
2. Whoa, _____ that fun - ky feel - in'. It's what you need to

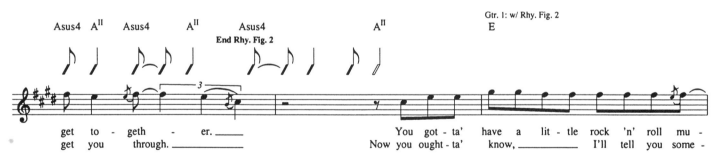

get to - geth - er. _____ You got - ta' have a lit - tle rock 'n' roll mu -
get you through. _____ Now you ought - ta' know, _____ I'll tell you some -

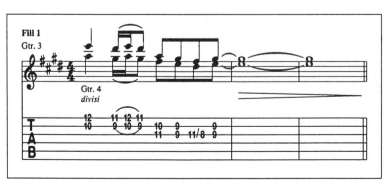

Feelin' Satisfied - 4 - 1

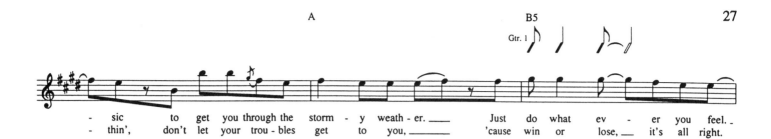

-sic to get you through the storm - y weath - er. ___ Just do what ev - er you feel.
-thin', don't let your trou - bles get to you, ___ 'cause win or lose, ___ it's all right.

When you don't know, ___ } noth-in's gon - na help you more than rock 'n' roll. ___ So come on! ___
When you let go, ___ }

Pre-Chorus

___ Now put your hands to-geth - er. ___ Yeah, come on! Put your hands to-geth - er. ___ Well, come on!

You know it's now or nev - er take a chance on rock ___ 'n' roll. _____

Breakdown

1. Ooh, are you read - y to - night?_
2. you, you can do what you like. _

2. It's up to

Ow! _

Ooh. _____

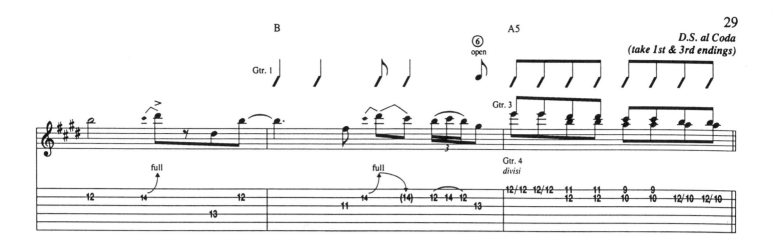

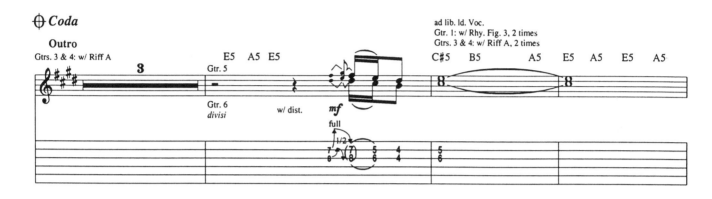

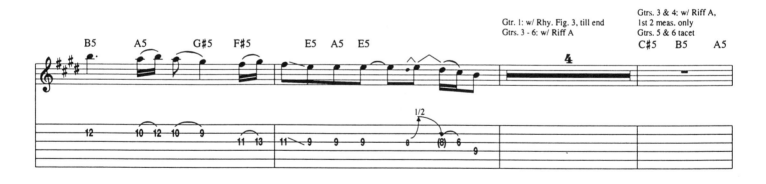

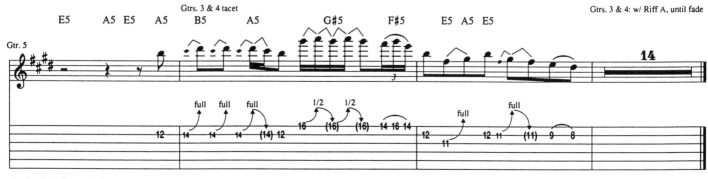

Feelin' Satisfied - 4 - 4

FOREPLAY

Words and Music by
TOM SCHOLZ

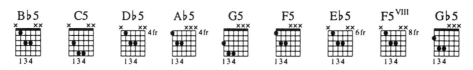

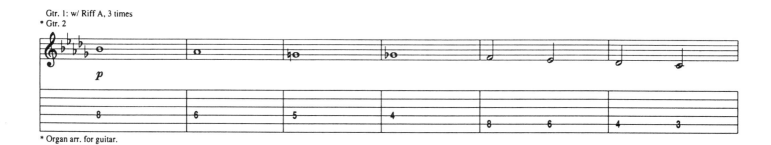

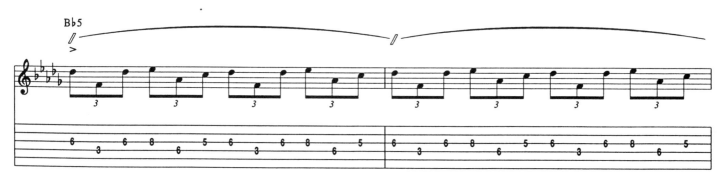

Foreplay - 4 - 1

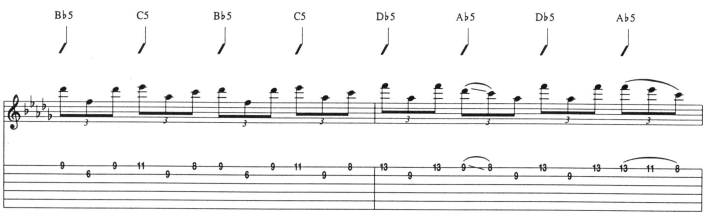

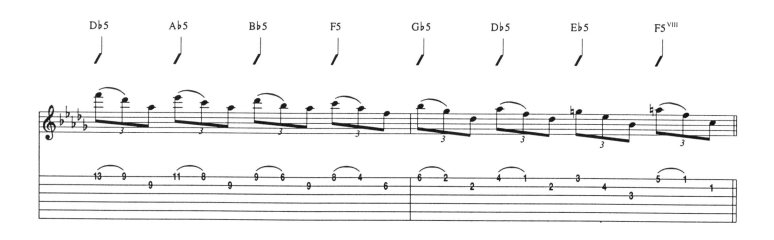

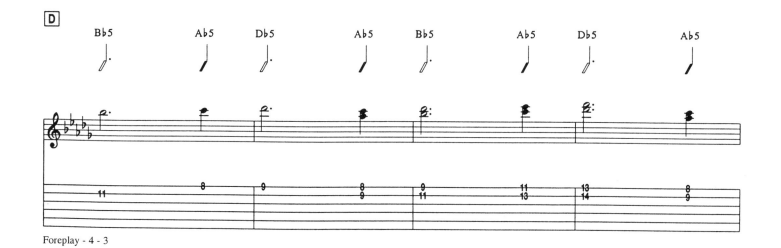

Foreplay - 4 - 4

HITCH A RIDE

Words and Music by
TOM SCHOLZ

Hitch a Ride - 6 - 2

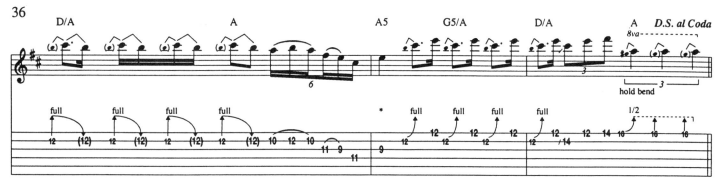

*Composite arrangement of two gtrs., next 2 meas.

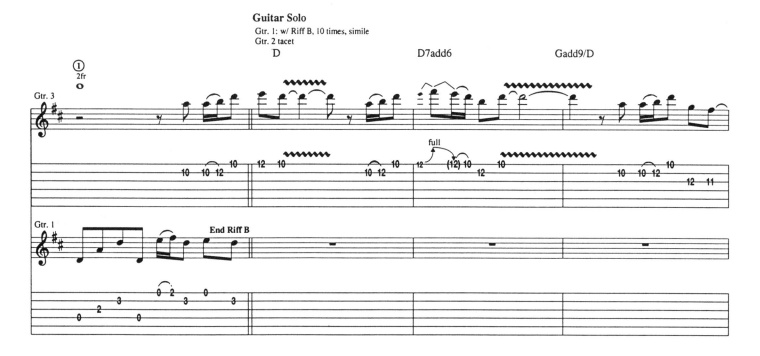

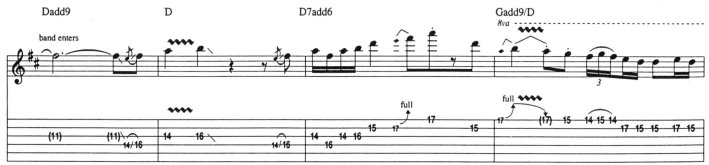

38

*Numbers to left of slash in TAB played by Gtr. 3

Additional Lyrics

2. Life is like the coldest winter.
People freeze the tears I cry.
Words of hell are minds I went to.
I've got to crack this ice and fly.

IT'S EASY

Words and Music by
TOM SCHOLZ

It's Easy - 8 - 1

It's Easy - 8 - 2

Pre-Chorus
Gtr. 2 tacet
Gtr. 4: w/ Riff A, 2nd time

'Cause when I get close ___ to you, ___ not ___ much to

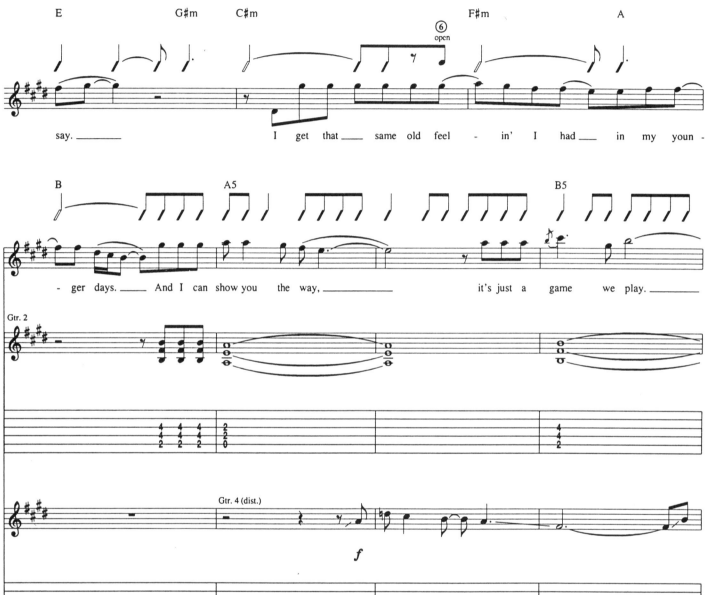

say. ___ I get that ___ same old feel - in' I had ___ in my youn -

- ger days. ___ And I can show you the way, ___ it's just a game we play. ___

Gtr. 2

Gtr. 4 (dist.)

Riff A
Gtr. 4 (dbld. w/ Bkgd. Voc.)
Gtr. 5
divisi

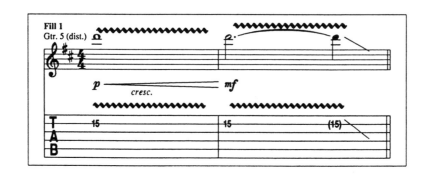

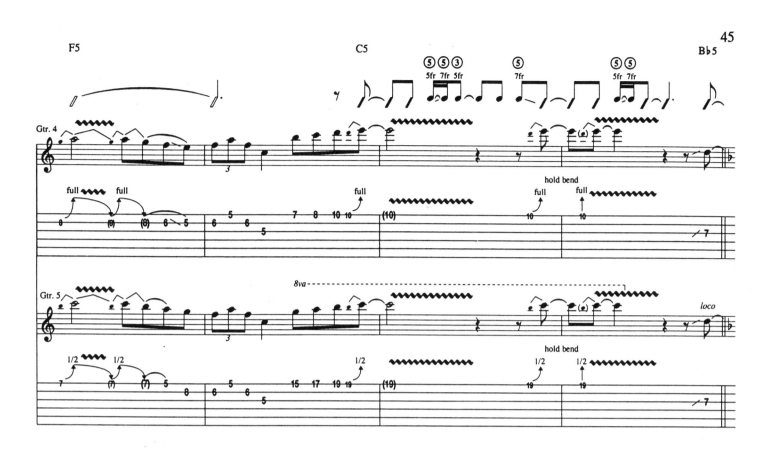

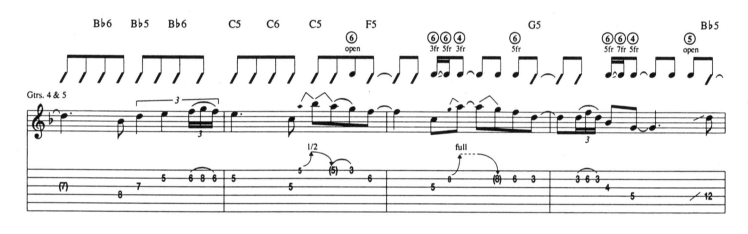

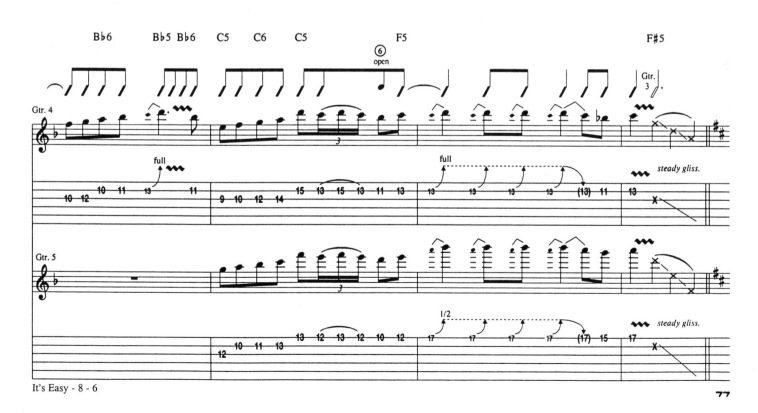

It's Easy - 8 - 6

Additional Lyrics:

2. Hey, you know I would concede,
And I think we both agree.
(You and I can testify that love is what we need.) Ah, hey!
Just take a look around you,
Livin' for the future is blind.
I believe what we achieve will soon be left behind.
The things that I try to say, are so hard to find.
When you doubt what your life is about let me ease your mind.

THE JOURNEY

Words and Music by
TOM SCHOLZ

The Journey - 2 - 1

LET ME TAKE YOU HOME TONIGHT

Words and Music by
BRAD DELP

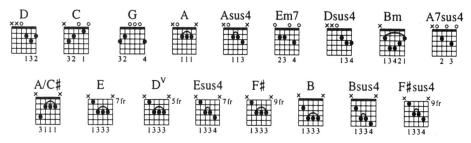

Intro

Slow Rock ♩ = 77

Let Me Take You Home Tonight - 5 - 1

%%S% **Chorus**

home to-night.____ Ma-ma now it's __ al-right.__ Let me take you

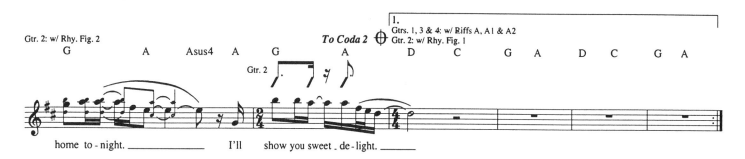

home to-night.____ I'll show you sweet _ de-light.__

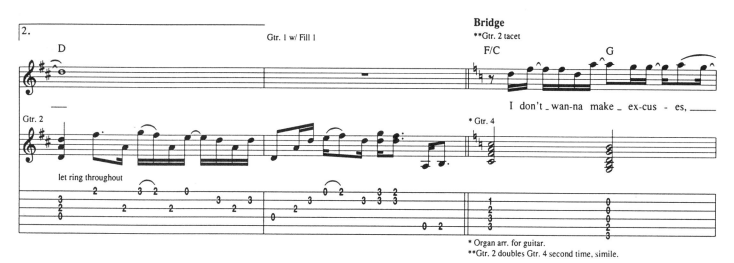

Bridge

I don't _ wan-na make _ ex-cus - es,____

* Organ arr. for guitar.
**Gtr. 2 doubles Gtr. 4 second time, simile.

To Coda 1

__ I don't wan-na lie.____ I've just got to get it loose.____

⊕ *Coda 2*

Outro

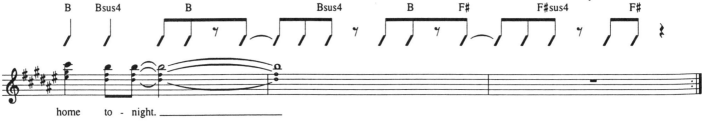

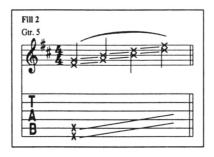

Additional Lyrics

2. You must understand this, I've watched you for so long
That I feel I've known you, I know it can't be wrong.

3. I don't wanna down you, I wanna make you high,
And I get this feeling whenever you walk by.

LONG TIME

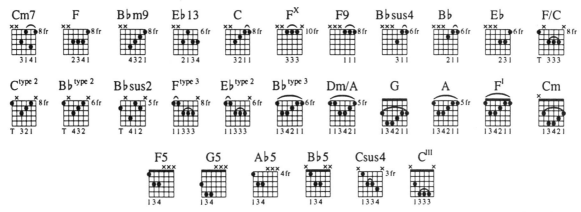

Words and Music by
TOM SCHOLZ

Intro

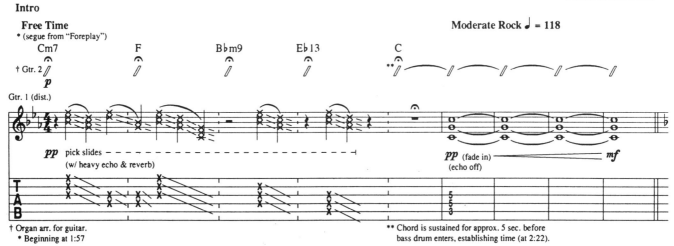

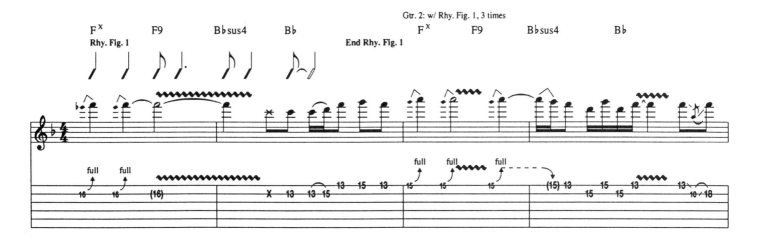

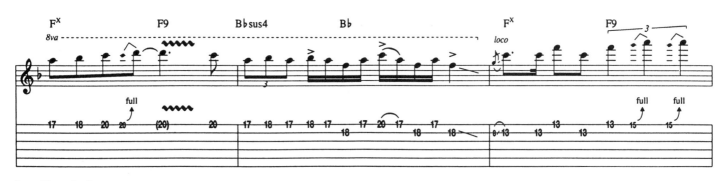

Long Time - 9 - 1

Verse

1. It's been such a long time, _____ I think I should be go - ing, ___ yeah. ___

___ Uh, time does - n't wait for me, _____ it keeps on roll - ing. _____

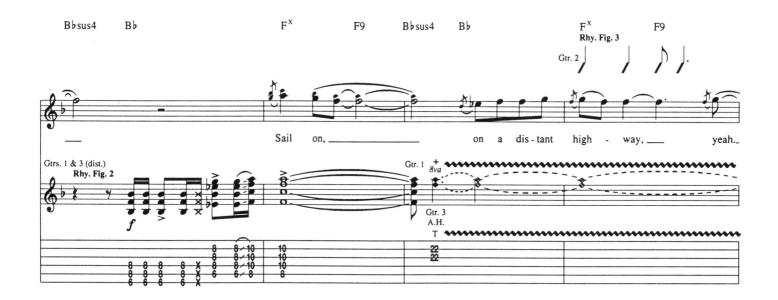

___ Sail on, _____ on a dis - tant high - way, ___ yeah. __

_____ I've got to keep on ___ chas - in' a dream, ___ I've got to be on my _____ way. _____

End Half-Time Feel

Guitar Solo

Gtr. 2: w/ Rhy. Fig. 1, 4 times
Gtr. 3: w/ Fill 1
Gtr. 4 tacet

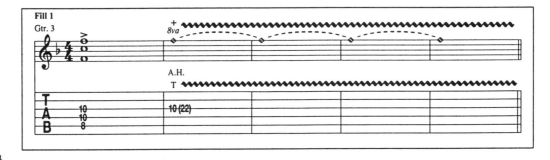

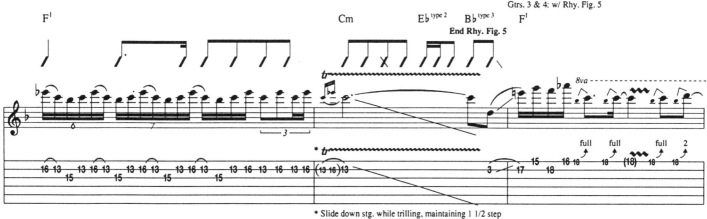

* Slide down stg. while trilling, maintaining 1 1/2 step
interval between notes. (Or dive w/ bar).

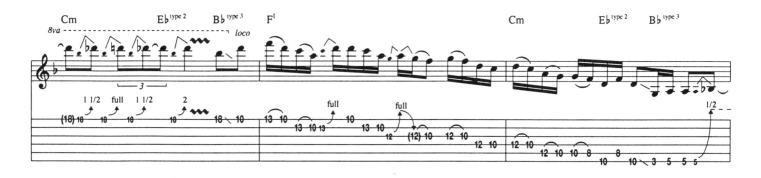

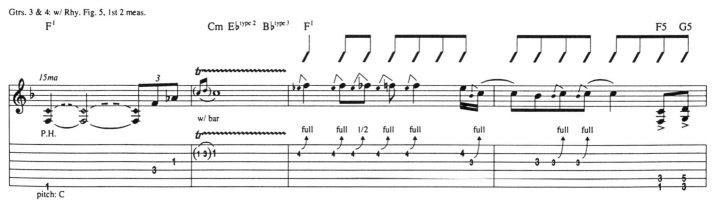

62

Long Time - 9 - 8

A MAN I'LL NEVER BE

Words and Music by
TOM SCHOLZ

A Man I'll Never Be - 8 - 1

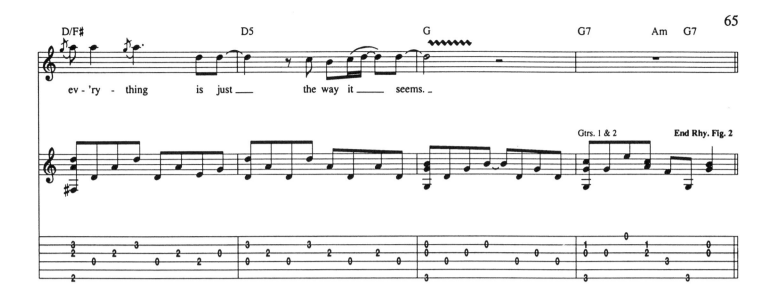

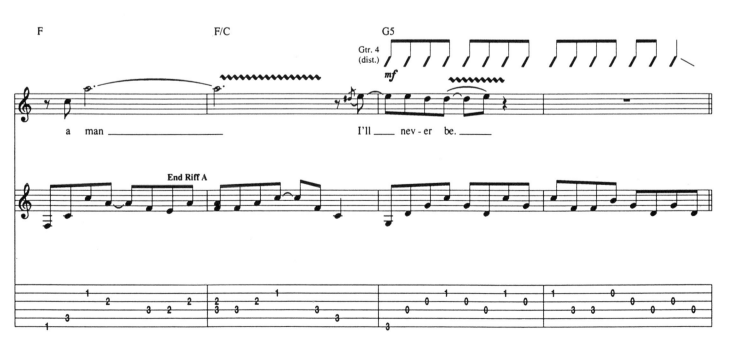

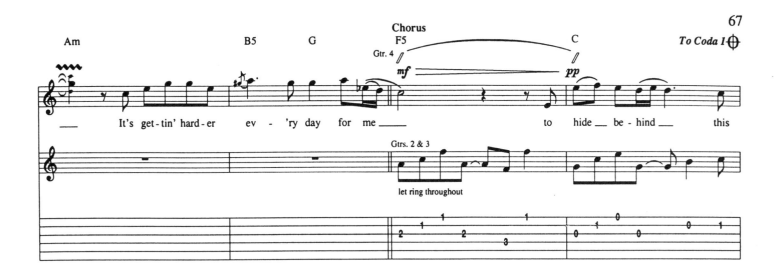

A Man I'll Never Be - 8 - 4

⊕ *Coda 1*

Guitar Solo

Additional Lyrics:

3. I can't get any stronger
   And I can't climb any higher.
   You'll never know just how hard I've tried.
   Cry a little longer and hold a little tighter.
   Emotions can't be satisfied.

A Man I'll Never Be - 8 - 8

MORE THAN A FEELING

Words and Music by
TOM SCHOLZ

play 3 times

Verse

3. When I'm tired ___ and think - in' cold, I hide in my mu - sic, for - get the ___ day. ___ And

dream of a girl ___ I used to know, ___ I close my eyes ___ and she slipped a - way. ___

PEACE OF MIND

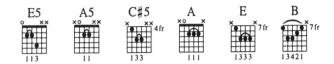

Words and Music by
TOM SCHOLZ

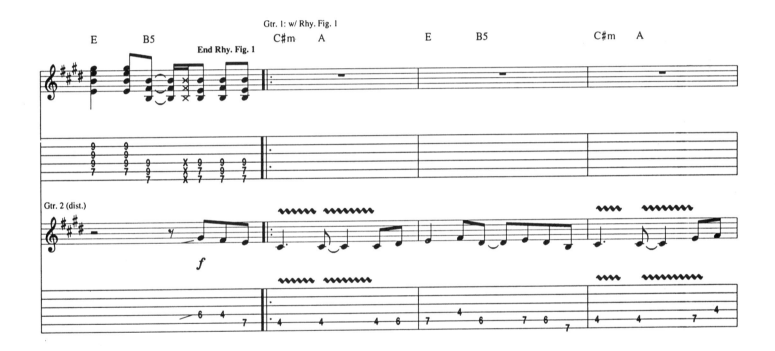

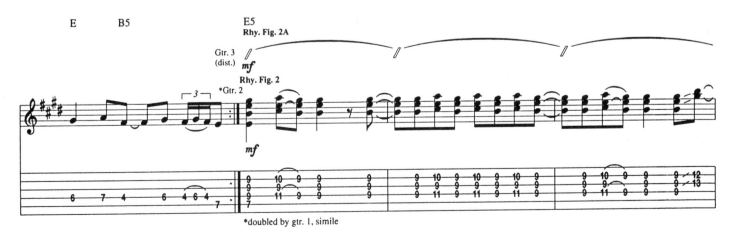

*doubled by gtr. 1, simile

Peace of Mind - 7 - 1

Yeah!   Whoa! _____   2. Now, you're

climb-in' to the top of the com-pa-ny lad-der, hope __ it does-n't take too __ long.__

__ Can't you see there'll come a day when it won't mat-ter, come __ a day when you'll be gone.__

Chorus

Whoa! _____ I un-der-stand __ a-bout __ in-de-ci-sion, __ but

I don't care __ if I get be-hind. __ Peo-ple liv-ing in com-pe-ti-tion.
(Ooh. _____)

All I want __ is to have my peace __ of __ mind. _____
(Ooh.)

pitch: B

Bridge

*pick scrapes

Peace of Mind - 7 - 3

PARTY

Words and Music by
TOM SCHOLZ and BRAD DELP

day af-ter day. I wan-na have some fun while I'm here. ___ I play the game when it's

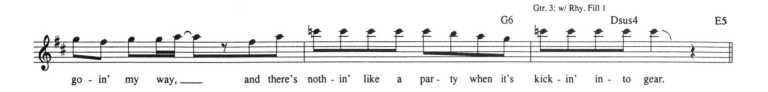

go-in' my way, ___ and there's noth-in' like a par-ty when it's kick-in' in-to gear.

Pre-Chorus

I'm get-tin' read-y for a par-ty to-night, yes, I'm get-tin' read-y to cruise. ___ And
3rd time: ('cause) (groove. ___)

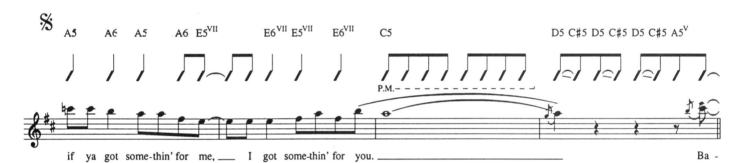

if ya got some-thin' for me, ___ I got some-thin' for you. ___ Ba-

Chorus

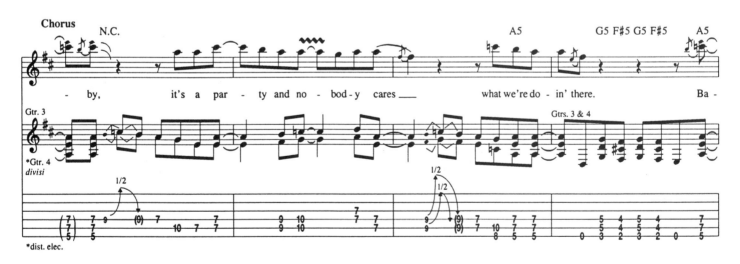

-by, it's a par-ty and no-bod-y cares ___ what we're do-in' there. Ba-

*dist. elec.

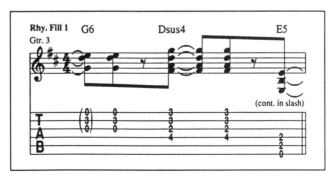

(cont. in slash)

Party - 6 - 2

Gtrs. 3 & 4: w/ Rhy. Figs. 3 & 3A, 3 times

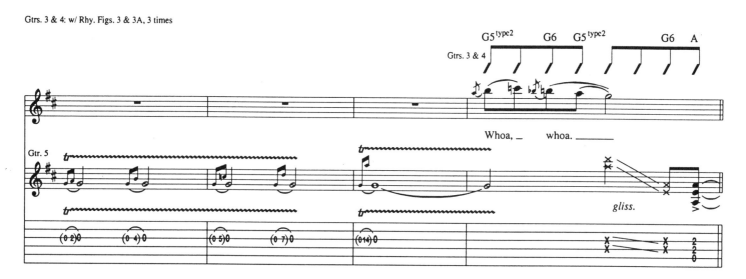

Whoa, __ whoa. _____

Verse

Gtr. 4 tacet
Gtr. 3: w/ Rhy. Fig. 1, 1 3/4 times

3. Get down and par-ty if ya need to. ___ Sure to find one in a crowd. ___ Ow!

D.S.S. al Coda 2

Gtr. 3: w/ Rhy. Fill 1

Just meet your friends and have a toke or two,___ in a place where they can nev-er play the mu-sic too loud.___

⊕ Coda 2

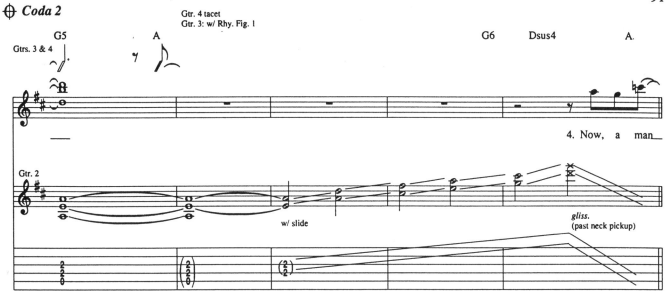

Verse

does-n't live on bread __ a - lone. __ You got - ta have some fun in each and ev - 'ry night. __ And a

wo-man got to have it if the truth be known. __ Let's get to - geth-er hon - ey it's all __ right. __ (I said uh,) (Come on!)

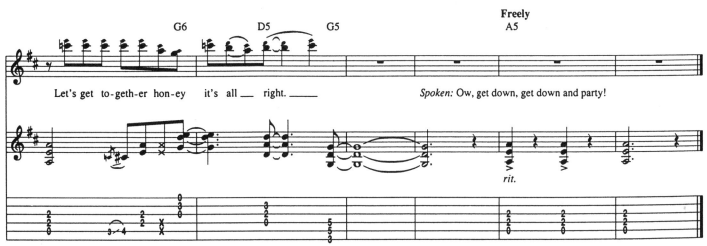

Let's get to - geth-er hon - ey it's all __ right. _____ *Spoken:* Ow, get down, get down and party!

ROCK & ROLL BAND

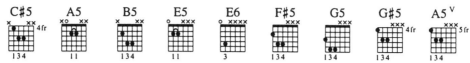

Words and Music by
TOM SCHOLZ

Rock & Roll Band - 5 - 1

3. Wait -

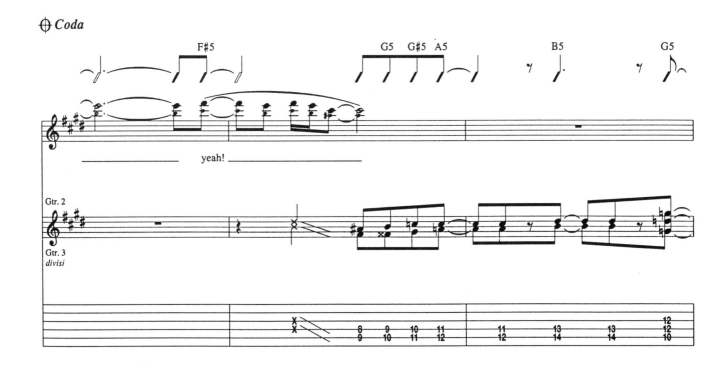

yeah!

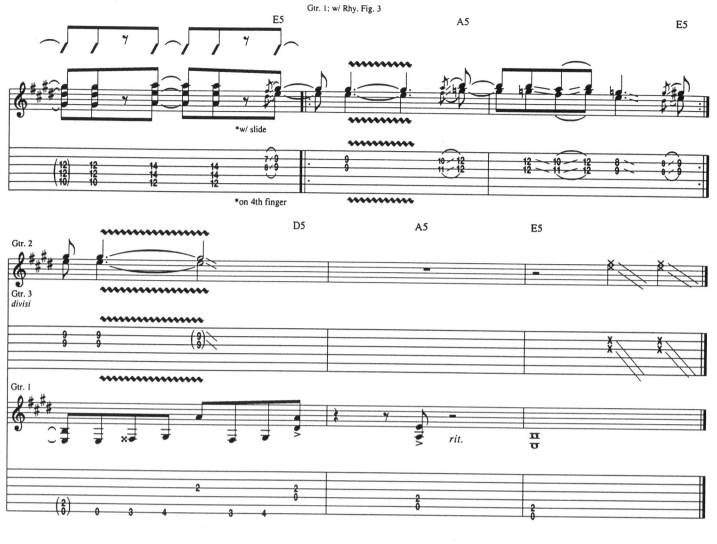

Additional Lyrics

2. Dancin' in the streets of Hyannis,
   We were getting pretty good at the game.
   People stood in line, they didn't seem to mind,
   Ya know everybody knew our name.
   Livin' on rock 'n' roll music,
   Never worry 'bout the thing we were missin'.
   When we got up on stage and got ready to play
   Everybody listened.

3. Playin' for a week in Rhode Island
   A man came to the stage one night.
   He smoked a big cigar and drove a Cadillac car
   And said, "Boys, I think this band's outta' sight."
   Signed a record company contract,
   You know I've got great expectations.
   When I hear you on the car radio
   You're gonna be a sensation.

SMOKIN'

Words and Music by
TOM SCHOLZ and BRAD DELP

Organ Solo

Gtr. 2

*Two guitars arr. for one.

Smokin' - 7 - 3

Gtr. 1: w/ Rhy. Fig. 4, 1st meas. only, 2 times
C5 D5
C5
G5 A5
D5
C5
A5
C5
Gtr. 1
8va
D5
C5
G5 type2
A5
(cont. in notation)
loco
Interlude
Gtr. 2 tacet
*Gtr. 3
Gm/A
Dm/A
A7sus4
A
Gtr. 1
Riff A
End Riff A
P.M.
w/ phaser
*Harpsichord arr. for guitar.
Gtr. 1: w/ Riff A
Dm/A
G7/A
Asus4
A
Gtr. 3 tacet
B♭5
A5
G5
Gtr. 1
*Gtr. 4
*Pipe organ arr. for guitar.
A5
B♭5
A5
G5
A5
10fr
8fr

Additional Lyrics

2. Get your feet on the floor, everybody rock and roll.
   Ya' got nothing to lose, just the rhythm and blues, that's all, yeah, no.
   Gonna feel okay, pick you up and take you away. Whoo!
   Get down tonight.

3. Everyone's jumpin', dancin' to a boogie tonight.
   Ah, clap your hands and your feet, or don't ya know it won't seem right, yeah.
   We're gettin' off today, we'll pick you up and take you away.
   Well, get down tonight, ya you know it.

SOMETHING ABOUT YOU

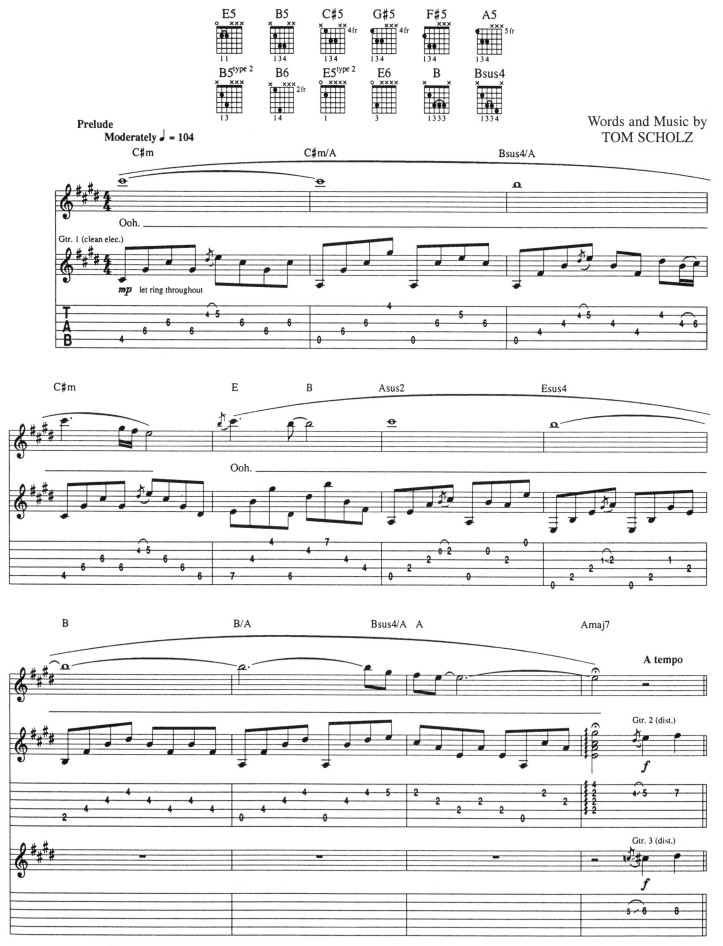

Words and Music by
TOM SCHOLZ

Something About You - 6 - 1

Outro

Additional Lyrics

2. When I get angry I say things I don't wanna say.
   I really mean it, I don't wanna leave you this way. Yeah, yeah.
   I couldn't help my reaction. (I didn't want you to know.)
   I lose control over you. (I don't want you to know.)

USED TO BAD NEWS

Words and Music by
BRAD DELP

*Keyboard arr. for gtr.

Used to Bad News - 5 - 1

Interlude

Gtrs. 1 & 2: w/ Riffs A & A1, 2 times

| D | D+9 | Fmaj7/D | | Gsus4 | G | D | D+9 |

Gon-na' find me a rea - son for sure.

| Fmaj7/D | Gsus4 | G | ***D.S. al Coda*** |

2. Don't tell me why

Coda

Gtrs. 1 & 2: w/ Rhy. Fill 2

| D | Dadd9 | | D | Dsus4 | D |

Yeah, yeah.

Keyboard Solo

G#m7   C#   C#m7

Gtrs. 1 & 2

Gtr. 3

| E | B | F# |

Bridge

G#m7   C#   C#m7   D

I know_ what you're say-in' is bad. It's not what I wan - ted but I'm rea-dy for that.

Rhy. Fill 2
Gtrs. 1 & 2

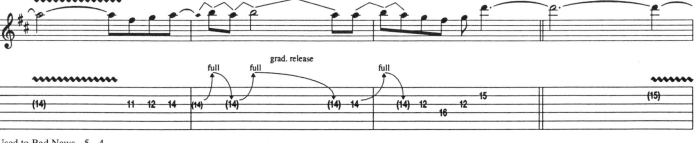

114

WE'RE READY

Words and Music by
TOM SCHOLZ

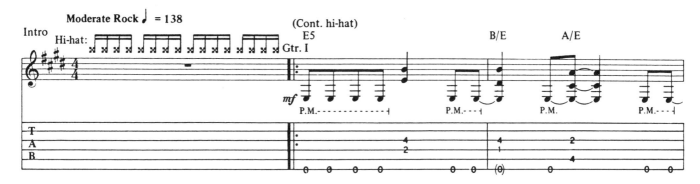

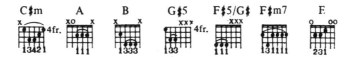

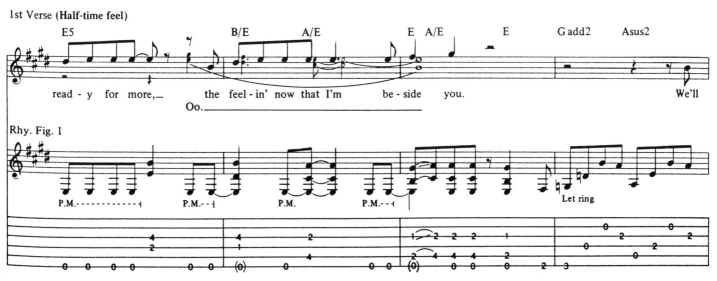

We're Ready - 9 - 1

116

We're Ready - 9 - 2

118

3rd Verse
w/Rhy. Fig. 1

ready now,   catch-in' a wave___ to ride on.
Oo.

Stead-y now,   head-in' where we___ de-
Oo.

cide.   on.___ And I know that there's some-thing that's just out of sight.

And I feel like we're try-in' to do some-thing right.

Come on, make it if we hold on tight,___ hold on tight.___ We're

Chorus

ready!   Yeah,_____ yeah!___ We're

ready!   Yeah,___ yeah!___ We're ready!   Hoo,___ hoo.___ We're

NOTATION LEGEND